SOMEWHERE

an anthology of poetry

Adrienne Tinn

2012

By the same author

With Different Eyes

To All My readers,

Once again a great thank you must be given to my husband Malcolm for listening patiently to my poems and for all his hard work in setting out this publication. It has taken a long time to produce this second anthology but after countless requests I have at last succumbed.

We have a local charity, Grove Cottage, that does a fantastic job in aiding children with special needs. I shall be sending a percentage of the proceeds from this anthology to help in the excellent work that they do.

Like the previous anthology, the poems cover a wide variety of subjects, among which are humour, nature, topical, fantasy and a little of the supernatural.

I hope you will enjoy them.

Adrienne

All rights reserved. No part of this publication may be reproduced, stored in a retrieval system or transmitted in any form or by any means, electronic, mechanical, photocopying, recording or otherwise without the prior permission of the publishers.

Published by HWW Publishing
c/o 65 Sheering Lower Rd
Sawbridgeworth
Herts CM21 9LG

First published 2012

ISBN 978-0-9560883-6-9

Typeset and cover design by Malcolm Tinn

Printed by Copyzone
Bishops Stortford CM23 3DY

Contents

Somewhere	1
Maytime River	2
Food, Inglorious Food	3
Rain	5
Bowling Along	6
Field of Dreams	7
Kerry Gems	8
A Night of Stars	10
Fox	11
Mischievous Mimi	12
Ritual Dance	13
Happy Cat	14
Gather the Strands	14
Early Autumn	15
The Return of Owl and the Pussycat	16
Ruby	18
Holy Island – Lindisfarne	19
Voices in the Air	20
A February Garden	21
No More Baked Beans	22
Miles Away from Anywhere	24
A Life in a Day	25
Over the Hill	26
Out of Time	27
Knickers	28
Tomorrow	29
My Betty	30
Sunrise at Niagara	31

Contents

Lynmouth	32
A Snow Day	34
An End and a Beginning	35
Magic Mushrooms	36
Web of Deceit	37
Mary Jane	38
A Bathtime Odyssey	39
I am Legend	41
Glendalough	42
A Potty Tale	43
A Summer Day	45
Stairway to the Stars	46
Light my Fuse	47
Bags and Baggage	48
Ilfracombe	51
A Slippery Trip	52
Beware the Juggernaut	53
Autumn of Life	55
Fireworks - Madeira	56
Blackie	58
They Say	59
Cockermouth	60
BBG Rats	61
A Brief Encounter	63
All Hallows Eve	64
Evening Walk in May	65
Grenada Island of Contrasts	67
The Charge of the White Brigade	69

Somewhere

Somewhere I shall find you…..
In early morning mist
Where dewdrops hang by silken threads
Each barely sunrise kissed;
Where birdsong greets with choral voice
The birthing of the day;
I'll look for you, I'll search for you
For you have gone away.

Somewhere I shall find you……
Among the bee-buzzed grass
Or through the forest's hidden paths
Where silent creatures pass,
Or near the brook that ripples on
And shows the way to go;
I'll seek for you, I'll call to you
And join the water's flow.

Somewhere I shall find you……
When evening shadows fall.
Was that your face that passed just now?
You did not heed my call.
I thought I knew the way you walked
And yet you moved on past.
I'll look once more and search for you
Though time is flying fast.

Somewhere I shall find you……
Perhaps within my dreams
Where worlds implode and time dissolves
And nothing's what it seems.
In that dark place I'll meet you.
You'll wipe away my pain
And I'll arise with youthful tread
And walk with you again.

Maytime River

The river ran through as rivers do
And a soft sun shone on the seated swan
Now still - at rest on her knitted nest
And a glimpse of brown was the early down
Of chicks who lay in the shade of may
While the cob hovered by proud head held high
And the river ran through as rivers do

Food, Inglorious Food

Umbrellas, raincoats, hats and wellies,
Great big bums and bulging bellies,
Wander through the teeming streets
Seeking out some luscious treats.

Ruby Tuesday, Subway, Hooters,
Eat while working at computers.
Tex Mex - noses twitch to savour
Wafted odours - chilli flavour.

Bagels fill the Bagel Bar -
Cream cheese, wallies from a jar.
In McDonalds burgers frying,
Children shouting, babies crying,

Beef or chicken, melted cheese,
Sauce and salad, what you please.
And what will come as no surprise -
Mountains of delicious fries.

Starbucks - here you're sure to find
Coffee drinks of every kind.
Ben and Jerry's - next door shop
Calling you to make a stop.

Ice cream melting on the tongue
Spooned inside by old and young.
Everywhere there's lots of seating
For you all to keep on eating.

Tossed aside all thoughts of caution -
Humankind of vast proportion
Waddle home to watch their tellies,
Great big bums and bulging bellies.

Moving on from day to day,
Munching all their lives away.

Rain

I hear the sound of the raindrop beat
When I'm snuggled up in bed
That pad-pad-pad on the roof above
Is a soft-shoe dance that I always love
As it echoes overhead

I've watched the waters building high
And seen the river race
The roar of the torrent that tears along
Is a liquid lion with its song
As it starts upon the chase

I've seen a single raindrop roll
Its way down the window pane
And find its path to the earth below
Where mighty waters swell and grow
To burst above again

I've turned my tongue to this liquid life
Have caught the drops as they fly
And watched the plants that had drooped of late
Stretch out their arms and stand up straight
To smile at a sunless sky

Bowling Along

Bowling along with the window wide
And a brisk breeze blowing
The rapeseed bright in the countryside
With gold heads glowing

Bowling along where the trees renew
All their spring coat glory
And birds sing out in the Maytime blue
Their new life story

Bowling along by the river-rush
With the proud swans gliding
Where reeds are rising tall and lush
And fleet fish hiding

Bowling along - comes a crash and thump -
Hear a front tyre rending
We have hit a pothole and a bump
That's our nice ride ending

Field of Dreams

Deceptive birdsong rising, falling
Harsh crescendo dying down
Distant voices crying, calling
Green to gold and gold to brown

Violent tempest tear me, draw me
Drag me down and hurl me high
Over roiling dust and maelstrom
Through a ruby blood-streaked sky

Rainfall burning, cooling, burning
Searing soothing sun-baked soil
Clutching comfort, earthward turning
Muddy bubbles burst and boil

Somewhere near harsh footsteps tramping
Ever onward, hear them pass
In my head a blaze of glory
In my hand a blade of grass

Kerry Gems

We sail across by ferry
Heading down to County Kerry
Through the Curragh of Kildare that racing scene
To the Shannon swiftly flowing
Sunlight setting waves to glowing
Passing fields of barley-brown and emerald green.

In Adare the castle towers
Look upon bright beds of flowers
And the roses still are blooming in Tralee
Where the windmill sails are turning
To remind us of the yearning
Of the folk once forced to sail across the sea.

From Killorglin to Killarney
It is all a load of blarney
For the little folk are hiding in the haze
Beneath treetops wildly tossing
'Beware Leprechauns are Crosssing'
Is painted on the signs to meet your gaze.

And the mountains tower over
Fields of fuchsia and clover
Where hawthorn berries hang like drops of blood
In the Dunloe Gap where only
Nature wild and stark and lonely
Still holds sway and rivers race away in flood.

In the distance in the morning
Mist descends there without warning
With Killarney's mountains hidden from our sight
And the rutting deer's wild bellow
Becomes muted then and mellow
In the cloudy covered lakeside morning light.

On occasion while out touring
We would shelter from the pouring
By a cosy fire in a wayside bar
With Guinness we'd be sated
With a shamrock decorated
Then carry on our cruising in the car.

But at last the break is ending
And homeward we are wending
Goodbye Killarney Cork and Dingle Bay
The songbirds chirp in chorus
And a rainbow shines before us
A fond farewell to guide us on our way.

A Night of Stars

I remember a night of stars
In a firmament pure and clear
Before the blanket that covered the sky,
Causing the plants to wither and die;
Smothering all in fear.

The stars, tiny twinkling gems,
In a heaven of midnight blue,
Before the deluge of fire and blood
Carpeting all in ashes and mud,
A sky where the birds once flew.

We used to love going out late,
The moon a solitary light.
But the moon has gone and the world is dark
And everywhere round is cold and stark
Struck with a terrible blight.

You taught me the names high above
And I learnt them all, in vain.
With one mighty flash and a pain-filled scream
We turned our Earth to a distant dream
And I'll not see them again.

I remember a night of stars
And you are a star now dear,
Far, far away in a place of your own.
And I sit at home in this world alone
With a sky that will never clear.

Fox

You prowl softly past to forage fields no more,
Plastic sacks and bins your urban haunts at night.
Across the lawn you leave your strong scented spoor -
A dew-misted trail in early morning light.

You also stalk the day - a dissipated fear
Of humans sees your snout dipped in thrown-out food.
Dispassionate your gaze, a twitched uncaring ear,
A mouth retaining succour for your waiting brood.

Red-coated creature where do you now call home?
No field or forest keeps you as in far-flown days.
Has urban ease seduced you, killed the need to roam?
Taught you how to scavenge and seek easy ways?

Calm, poised, waiting - there is beauty in your stance.
A twitching of the brush on your red-furred rear,
A swivel of your head, a swift cold-eyed glance
A paddy-pad of paws as you disappear.

Mischievous Mimi - September 2009

In skin-warmed vest and pants
White, stark against her sun-browned body,
She bounces cheerfully out of the porchway
In greeting.
"Come Granny," she says
In authoritative four-year-old voice
And, hand fast-clasped in mine,
 Pulls me swiftly forward.
"Come let me show you in."

The early evening air now autumn-cooled,
Follows us through the house
In breeze-blown gusts.
"Miffy," she says and points -
Then, light as a fairy, flits her way above,
Tiptoeing to climb her teetering tower of toys
To stand beside the outstretched cat
Who, seated in dubious safety
On the fish tank's mottled top,
Watches his tiny mistress
With slitted green-gold eyes.

"Nice Miffy," she repeats with mischievous smile.
The cat lies still and stares.
Her fur, at last regrown
Is silky in its glossy blackness.
There's little now to show, that not so long before
In misty morning frantic fervour,
The tiny hand that strokes,
Had soaped and shaved her pet.

Ritual Dance

Starlings wheel over the fields of dead clover -
A ritual dance in an autumn-grey sky
Climbing and crying the old year is dying
Wing-tipping branches while swooping on by

In v-line they feather the dull dismal weather
Then circle and soar in a wave of delight
Diving and falling their dark message calling
Then zoom back on high and away out of sight

Happy Cat

Happy cat seated here
Cradled safe on master's chair;
No cruel world you need to fear
With danger lurking everywhere.

For you, the comfort that you crave
Good food and cream at every meal;
No need to fight to prove you're brave;
No need to slyly slink or steal.

You came one night through rain and storm
And moaned and mewed outside our door.
We brought you in and kept you warm
And vowed you'd never suffer more.
Now queen of all whom chance has sent
You may rest here in warm content.

Gather the Strands

Walk around the web of my world
In calm concentric circles
Gather the strands in your comforting hands
And draw them gently in until
You pull them taut - so very tight
That you block out the cold white light
And fill my heart my very soul
With a welcoming warmth
That makes me whole.

Early Autumn

Among the shifting swansong shadows
a cool September breeze blows
late summer's detritus of ochred leaves
across the shaven lawn

A glossy grey dove wings swiftly
over the few late roses
that colour the leaf-greened pergola

A solitary butterfly flutters above the hedge
searching for who knows what
as ash leaves run in ripples
against the white-blue sky

The bamboo sways above the trellis
in undulating delicate dance
while bird-bath waters wafted by the wind
await their feathered friends

The newly-pink weigela and lavender purple-grey
wash the nearby bed with colour
as storm clouds dull the day

I shiver in the autumn wind
and butterfly myself away

The Return of Owl and the Pussycat
(with apologies to Edward Lear)

The owl and the pussycat sailed back home
In their beautiful pea-green boat.
They'd eaten the honey and lost all the money
Wrapped up in the five pound note.
The owl looked off to the distant east
And sang to the soft guitar,
"Oh horrible pussy, oh pussy you beast,
What a hard wicked pussy you are, you are, you are,
What a hard wicked pussy you are."

Pussy said to the owl, "You silly old fowl
How awfully bad you sing.
We're no longer married. That burden I've carried
Has gone and I've sold up the ring."
So they sailed back fast to their distant past
From the land where the bong tree grows
And tried to forget the snakes and the wet
And the pig with the ring on his nose, his nose, his nose,
And the pig with the ring on his nose.

The pig who was willing to sell for one shilling
His ring, stole their money and ran.
They saw him rush off with the turkey and scoff
As the two raced away in a van.
Pussy gobbled the mince and chewed up the quince
And cast off the runcible spoon.
Now she eyed up the owl, that gullible fowl
As they sailed by the light of the moon, the moon, the moon,
As they sailed by the light of the moon.

Ruby

Here comes Ruby, lightly tripping,
Moves so swiftly - almost skipping,
Head thrown back and dark hair swinging,
People turn to hear her singing.
In the springtime of her days
Ruby jokes and laughs and plays.

Ruby takes the children with her,
Shopping day, no time to dither,
Hair pinned back and somewhat slower,
Figure rounded, voice tones lower.
In the summer of her life,
Carer, mother, helper, wife.

College days are now long ended
And far-flung the brood she tended,
Tinted hair but joints are achy,
Lifting things she's rather shaky,
Early in the evening, sleepy,
Autumn-time is somewhat weepy.

Ruby's wheelchair at the crossing,
Ruby's thoughts of dark curls tossing,
Grey-haired, mitted, as is seeming,
Wrinkled eyelids closed for dreaming.
In the winter of her years
Slowly creeping, two small tears.

Holy Island – Lindisfarne

These waters whisper memories
Held deep on Lindisfarne
And grasses quiver beside the tarmac road

Above the pale green marshland by the causeway
A wind sends ripples shivering along
While a seabird dips and dives in search of food

In the distance pale green humps along its back
The island waits
A holy place no more
No sandalled footsteps tread its lonely shore
No tonsured head is bowed in silent prayer

A castle-fortress built to guard the bay
Grey stone and stark
Looks down on silver lapping waves

Along the stone-strewn beach below
Clouds scud swiftly past
And a pigeon pecks at seeds and grasses
Upon the pebbled paths

Perhaps at night a phantom footstep treads
Its lonely watch along the battlements
Seeking for foreign foes
then slowly fades with morning mists
Into the distant past
And memories held deep on Lindisfarne

Voices in the Air

Voices scatter on the wind-whipped air
Curl about the treetops shimmer in the sky
Lightly laugh their way to Heaven spreading everywhere
Crawling over puffball clouds dancing on up high

Voices stifled in the heat-hazed air
Slide in slow soft rhythm circle round your head
Sinuous snakelike seeking solace anywhere
Congregate together then flee with tiptoe tread

Voices shiver in the brittle air
A stone-cold silver symphony with icicles at play
Batter bare brown branches in infinite despair
Shatter into silence and sadly slip away

A February Garden (2009)

Yesterday two tiny snowdrops stood,
Sheltered by the haircut-holly tree
Among its brittle, brown and littered leaves,
Beside soft shoots that parted soil to see.

The winter sun set in a summer sky,
Bright blue and cloudless, sent a dappled light
Through bare, bowed branches to the earth beneath
And on the two bent heads of creamy white.

Ceramic toadstools' mottled colours shone
Where ivy crawled and ornamental grass
Rustled in the wind and whispered low,
"Appreciate this time. It soon will pass."

Today, awake into a world of white -
A coverlet that cushions all around.
The birds stay sheltered in their hawthorn home -
No morning chorus – snow has muffled sound.

Our bird bath is a giant ice cream cone.
The big bronze heron sports a fancy hat.
No sign of snowdrops, they are buried deep;
Neither paw-prints of the neighbour's cat.

The garden in a solemn silence sleeps;
Just one poor pigeon his lone vigil keeps.

No More Baked Beans

Each evening comes the call to tea,
"Baked beans on toast tonight!"
Those orange blobs on burnt brown bread -
I hate the bloody sight!

The opener carves up the tin.
They splat as out they drop.
That simmering, the sickly smell,
The bubble and the pop.

The knife that tussles with the toast,
The fork that grips each lump,
The sauce that slithers down my chin
Gives me the blooming hump.

At school they call me Rumbletum.
I know the reason why!
They hold their nose as I walk past
And look up to the sky.

It's not my fault. I hate the stuff.
For choice I'd eat no more.
But every day it waits for me
As I come through the door.

I had a dream the other night.
My mum stood, pan in hand,
"I've two tins here for you my love.
Now aint that really grand?"

I grimaced and I turned my back,
"Dear mum, you cannot stay!"
Pulled down my jeans, erupted loud
And blew her clean away.

Miles Away from Anywhere (Poland 1941)

It was miles away from anywhere
In a golden new-grassed glade,
Where sunlight tipped the treetops
And scattered into shade

That I heard the gentle whispers
As they wafted round my head -
Voices I remembered
From those I knew, now dead;

Felt the touch of ghostly fingers
That gently swept my face,
Miles away from anywhere
In that silent, sleepy place.

Then a thousand phantom footsteps
Slid softly through the grass
With the light, low lilt of laughter
As I watched their shadows pass.

And my mother's voice was singing
The song that only we
Both knew from days of childhood
When all the world was free.

But the fumes of fear awoke me
And my gold world turned to grey
When they beat with clubs and truncheons
And stole my clothes away

Then machine guns rattled round us
And screaming rent the air
And I fled into the ether -
Miles away from anywhere.

A Life in a Day

The butterfly wafts lightly past
delicate wings a-flutter.
Why is this creature named that way -
a fly made out of butter?

Alighting gently on a plant
it touches; flits away,
skipping on from leaf to leaf,
the life dance of a day.

Flitter, flutter, fly of butter,
blend into the sky.
Melt on into nothingness.
Where do you go to die?

Over the Hill

Over the hill where the grasses blow
And tall trees stand in the evening glow
Casting long shadows that begin to grow,
I must make my way.

In pre-sleep dreaming the music comes -
Birdsong, bee-song in tonal hums -
Soft with the sound of some distant drums
At the end of day.

Shapes move towards me - I know them all -
The night folk are waiting to hear my call,
Those from the past that I loved and recall
But they will not stay.

Old wrinkled faces are smoothed again.
Carefree the bodies that were racked with pain.
I call to them softly, 'Stay here please remain
Do not fade away.'

But dreams are so fleeting, though they smile at me,
Sleep draws them backwards to infinity,
Back up that hillside, dim and shadowy,
Distant shades of grey.

Out of Time

His world a million miles away
A tiny twinkling light
Rested on the bosom of the sky
Comets bright-tailed passed in play
Like brilliant birds in flight
Dancing in the Heavens way up high

So long so long since he had left
To travel out in Space
Searching for he knew not what nor where
Now despondent and bereft
He yearned to leave this place
To seek the soothing comfort of the air

He'd seen enough of war and blood
Of greed and hate and fear
Tiny children left to fend alone
He'd found his way through famine flood
And wiped away the tear
That trickled slowly downward on its own

He sought the silent firmament
Where solitary he
Could dance around the stars in sheer delight
Eradicate the time he spent
With Earth's sad family
And revel in the rhythm of the night

Knickers

The bloomers blowing on the line
Ballooned there wild and free.
And with their legless high-kick dance
Those words came back as if by chance
My Grandma said to me:-

"When I was young, my little lass,
Our knicker-legs hung low.
Elastic clung beneath the knees;
We weren't allowed to swing or tease
Or put our bums on show.

And only cotton, white as white
And starched - perhaps a frill -
To cover up our naughty parts,
They caused no tremor to men's hearts
No tingling or thrill.

The only satin ones we saw
Were in that can-can dance.
Oh all those flounces, silk and lace
Brought looks of envy to our face;
We would have loved the chance.

We got some silk. The war did that
When parachutes came down.
We'd grab the chance and sew and snip
Make cami-knickers and let rip
And live it up in town.

Long live the sexy underwear
That's waiting there for you!
Wear frilly panties or a thong
But please don't wear your knickers long
Like we once had to do.

Tomorrow

I'll do all the washing tomorrow
and polish the windows as well.
I'll hunt for dust on the topmost shelves
where so many ornaments dwell.
I'll clear up the post in my office
and stack all the papers away.
But nothing will get done tomorrow
for tomorrow will be today.

My Betty

She's my special sweaty Betty
And she looks just like a Yeti
I could throw her off the jetty
In the sea.

For she is so big and bumpy
With a nose both round and lumpy
And a stare that makes me jumpy
Here at tea.

I would love to stop her gawking
And the way she's always talking;
Say to her when we're out walking,
"Come with me."

Then together with dog Rover
Drive her to the Cliffs of Dover
Give a shove and push her over
Happily.

Still I sit and watch her lunching
Loudly laughing while she's crunching
Dribbling bits as she is munching
Noisily.

****

Joy - there's no more noisy snoring
And no incessant jawing
For she's lying 'neath the flooring
Silently.

Sunrise at Niagara

Wide waters wend their way to Horseshoe Falls
Where sunrise paints the sky in red and grey.
And seagulls mill in hundreds with wild calls -
Black dots upon the rainbow clouds of day.
The river gathers speed between the banks,
Drawing on water from the wider lake
To pour past trees that stand in serried ranks,
A massive sweep that makes the treetops shake.
The power of the Falls begins to grow,
Lit by an orange sun that starts its climb
Above wild rivulets that tipped with snow
Dance to their drop and fall in furious time,
Then, in a mad white mass of mist and foam
Rage, roaring down to meet a calmer home.

Lynmouth - (The flood August 1952)

In Lynmouth the rivers wind
Soft susurration
Sibilant whispers that murmur and mutter
Where the wild waters once
Shocked a whole nation
With fierce foaming fury
And death and destruction
A mad racing torrent of pure devastation

August the summer month
Rain kept on falling
Tears from a heaven whose cold constant weeping
Battered and beat at banks slithering seeping
Rivulets grew to streams
These that flowed gently
Joined in a mighty mass silently creeping
Dancing then running rushing and roaring
An almighty surging a giant outpouring

And down it came down it came
All without warning
Malevolent massive a rabid rampaging
From deep in the night to that cold early morning
A forty foot wall of death howling and raging

And frenzied it bore along all it encountered
Easy to haul and prise boulders of giant size
Out of their resting place into this mighty race
Trees were no obstacles bridges and houses
Walls burst and fell apart
Mother and tiny child
Caught in the torrent's wild
Ferment its mighty heart
Bearing them easily down to the surging sea
Thirty four died that night
In the flood's fearsome flight

Fifty years on I stand watching the waters flow
Running round tiny rocks singing on soft and low
Soft susurration
Whispers say, "Don't forget Nature has power yet"
Above where the rivers play a seagull soars on its way
Borne on the gentle breeze
High above verdant trees
Into the bright blue of day

A Snow Day

Snow, a glowing wonderland - a gleaming world of white,
A winter coat of cladding for the trees,
Where flakes cling close together in the cold December light
And glisten as they gather up to freeze.

A paradise for children sleighing swiftly down the hill,
Or snowball fighting in the icy air,
Or arms outstretched in balance with no thought to winter chill
Sliding freely forward without care.

A blanket over bushes where birds at home inside,
Huddle up for warmth with muted voice,
Pop out to peck at peanuts, the frozen ground untried -
With berries hidden deep they have no choice.

While on the icy pavement with wary booted tread,
People walk the dog or wend their way,
Dodging icy patches as they search with bended head
For safety on this bright white winter day

An End and a Beginning

A bright star flared an instant in the firmament
Lighting up the heavens all around
The people stared in wonder
As it ripped the world asunder
A flashing flaming fury without sound

A wild atomic power winged relentlessly
Singing one shrill note of purest tone
A brilliant bird of glory
With no man to tell the story
Leaving Earth a nothingness unknown

An inky blackness in a starlit firmament
Awaits another blast of purest light
An end and a beginning
A losing and a winning
Decillions of days to follow night

Magic Mushrooms

Mighty, magic mushrooms
Stand beneath the trees
Topped with satin, rounded heads
That greet the wayward breeze
Multi-tones of golden browns
And iridescent blue
Turquoise melting into green
And reds of deepest hue

Whose smell can cause descent to Hell
Or shoot you high to touch the sky
Then melt down low to feel the glow
Of tongue-tilt flames that twist and turn
Whose ice-fire-flickers beat and burn
And tear apart your very heart

The fiery flood of bursting blood
Spreads around without a sound
Creates a pool that starts to cool

Then mushroom tongues of purple-pink
Dart out in dance and start to drink
And as they sup begin to grow
To giant-size and cast a glow

You leave your body spiral high
Like wood-smoke reaching for the sky
Like shining stars - stream out disperse
Your being to the universe

And as you circle round and fly
You see so far below
Enchanted mounds of magic mushrooms
Glisten gleam and glow

Web of Deceit

Twisting contorting and endlessly spinning
Turning cavorting no end or beginning
Climbing and dropping in patterns unending
Fine shining filaments endlessly tending
Dewdrops at daybreak each caught and collected
Spectrum of colour in sunlight reflected

Network of beauty
Awaiting its duty
Silk threads enfolding
Clasping and holding
A gift for the creature
Of delicate feature
Who waits at the centre
For those that might enter

Who readily greets them
And steadily eats them

Mary Jane

My name is Mary Jane,
Daughter of the sun,
Lush and ripe, I'm at my best
Sheltered close to man's warm breast,
A vessel full of fun.

He wants what I can give,
His partner of the day,
Euphoric, he caresses me,
Cradling - anxiety
Lest I should steal away.

I hear from deep within
The rapid beating drum.
I smile to see what I can do
To hearts, to cause this wild tattoo
And see what more may come.

So many parts am I;
Such power I can wield.
They give to me their heart and soul
I spit them out no longer whole.
Come pick me from the field.

A Bathtime Odyssey

(From news of a container of bathtime toys that were washed overboard in the Pacific Ocean, some of which are being washed up on the coast of N. Scotland and from whom scientists can understand the cyclical 'spin' of water on the sea's surface. A gyre is a large circular current system which gathers debris on the sea surface.)

Twenty eight thousand plastic toys are floating on the sea -
Overboard they tip together falling fast and free.
From Hong Kong they try to float towards the USA
But in the North Pacific Ocean sadly lose their way.

Ducks and turtles, frogs and beavers bobbing round and round
In the freezing Arctic oceans where the ice is found.
In the gyres they toss and tumble, rock and roll and race,
Skim the surface of those seas and try to leave that place.

Dip goodbye to one another - some traverse the tide,
Navigate the Bering Straits, a long and lonesome ride.
Passing fish in blank amazement eye this motley crew,
Then look on until they've gone and sailed to pastures new.

Frogs and beavers, ducks and turtles do their merry dance,
Caught in every passing current, moved along by chance.
Up and down the waves they slide and slither as they go -
On their painted plastic bodies slime and seaweed grow.

Then they drift apart - no more a mixed and merry band.
One lone frog sails slowly up and settles on Uig Sands
In the Outer Hebrides - ten thousand miles he's done.
Now scientists can chart the spin of water from his run.

Bold, brave froggie, single sailor, first one of his kind
Impatiently awaits them all - the friends he left behind -
The odyssey of bathtime toys that teach us of the sea,
Frogs and turtles, ducks and beavers floating fast and free.

I am Legend

I am the one that walks the night
When moonlight shines on wind-washed trees;
Whose bright hair turns from red to gold
To swirl in snake-dance with the breeze;
Who never will grow old.

I am the one with milk-white skin -
The nymph of dreams and man's desire
Of rounded limbs, curvaceous form,
Who sets alight the body's fire -
A siren of the storm.

I am the one whose dark eyes cause
A very vortex in the mind;
Who delves the depths to seek the soul,
Devour, depart and leave behind
My prey no longer whole.

I am the one whose laugh is heard
Above the ocean's wildest waves;
Who sings the songs that lure below
To sandy depths and shell-strewn graves
Where seaweed grasses grow.

I am Legend! - I the one
Who sails the sky on windswept nights;
Who casts a shadow on the moon
And makes the owls screech loud with fright.
Beware! I'll be there soon.

Glendalough

Down near the river in Glendalough
The children's swings swung to and fro
But no breeze blew where the roses grew
And no feet trod by the water flow
Soft shivers rippled through the air
By the soft stream music running there

I watched the rhythm of the swings
As unseen youngsters played their games
Then by my ear I seemed to hear
"Just ask of us we'll tell our names"
I quickly turned to give reply
But no-one stood on the grass nearby

And swifter higher moved the swings
Till I thought they'd break and fly away
A laugh a call a scream a fall
A child's voice stilled at the end of play
In Glendalough by the tree-greened hill
Where the water wept and the air was still

A Potty Tale

I'm sitting in my Jargo up in space,
Steering like a madman in a race,
Dodging asteroids and comets
My ears plugged up with grommets
While noisy vessels whistle past my face.

I'm a jargonaut who loves his astral work
And the danger bit is just an extra perk.
When those Frenemies surround me
I will always look around me
To check the Black Hole shadows where they lurk.

My Jargo pet sits huggled by my side.
It's happy when I take it for a ride -
With silky legs akimbo
It stares into the limbo
With eyes like two large ducks' eggs lightly fried.

I hear it squeak, "Meh, meh," as round we zoom,
While other Jargos lurk there in the gloom,
When with noise like stellar thunder
A galactic great Gesunder
Approaches as its wide-mouthed cannons boom.

"A chamber pot is flying in the sky,"
I tell my pet and look him in the eye.
His wording somewhat alters -
"Oui, oui," his small voice falters
And trembles as the tracer bullets fly.

But I let loose an anti-potty shell
Which blows it up with a disgusting smell.
The thunderbox disperses
With meteoric curses
And we fly off assured that all is well.

A Summer Day

The smell of new-mown grass wafts through the air
While sunshine gleams on bush and hedge and tree.
The birds trill loud as though they wish to share
Their music on a Summer day with me.

Fine, fluffy clouds slide slow across the sky
Of palest blue that wanders into white.
Creamy clover and golden buttercups
Spread their petals to the warming light.

A welcome breeze blows flower, leaf and fern.
A bee alights for nectar on a flower.
I feel there is so much that we could learn
From Nature's stillness yet its giant power.

The fountain ripples on and droplets fall.
A cloud crawls over hiding sun away.
I revel in the sound of songbirds' call
And magic of an English Summer day.

Stairway to the Stars

I see you sailing through the Milky Way
Your cheeks with colour and your eyes ablaze.
Finally finished with your Earthly stay
You curl in the ether of astral rays.

Your body now painless and weightless - free
To float like a feather where nothing bars
What you might touch and you might see,
Climbing high on the Stairway to the Stars.

Light my Fuse

Light up my fuse and set me on fire
Watch as the sparks ignite higher and higher
Fathom the ferment follow the flame
Gravitate oscillate into the game
Energise elevate Heaven aspiring
Potent omnipotent lustful desiring
Quicksilver jetting intensification
Shooting out foaming forth wild excitation
Falling to Earth succumb to deflation
Replete now in Lethe's annihilation

Bags and Baggage

I've lost my bags and baggage
All disappeared like that -
My back was turned one minute -
It's left me cold and flat

My passport and my wallet
Stuffed full of nice new cash
Was snapped up in a second
And vanished in a flash

I let that girl persuade me
I met her just by chance
We both were sitting at the bar
I asked her for a dance

With figure sleek and slinky
Her dark eyes asked for more
She told me in the bedroom
She came from Singapore

Her voice was like soft music
Her lips like ruby wine
Her skin was soft smooth velvet
Her figure was divine

She'd come to make her fortune
But now that she'd met me
She'd change her plans and settle
In Burnham by the Sea

We walked the beach together
The wind whisked her black hair
But sometimes on her lovely face
I saw a saddened stare

I asked what was the problem
The tears welled in her eyes
She missed her family and friends
This came as no surprise

I said we'd have a holiday
We'd fly to Singapore
She danced with glee and held me tight
A great night was in store

I organised the travel
The money we might need
Her eyes lit up – A little More -
Surprising signs of greed

We got to Euston Station
The crowds welled all about
I placed my luggage on the ground
I heard my sweet one shout

I turned at the commotion
One moment was enough
She darted off and left me
She whipped away my stuff

I've lost my bags and 'baggage'
My wallet's far away
I'll trust no other woman
Until my dying day

Ilfracombe

On grey-skied summer's day the seagulls swoop
With raucous cries above the windswept sea.
While in the harbour waiting for the tide,
The boats tug at their chains to be set free
To ride the rollers, dance in unity.

Above the bay, flag flying far aloft,
A chapel stands, of solid rough-hewn stone,
Where late at night the lantern gave its glow,
A warning to brave sailors out alone,
A guiding light to safety, surely shown.

The shop fronts' gaudy colours stand out bright.
In one, where home-made fudge is being sold,
Its golden mixture glistens in the light,
The wooden battens pat and push and fold
This sugar heaven, home into its mould.

Past Cornish pasties, souvenirs, cream teas,
Between short showers towards the quay I go.
The waves slap soft against the stone sea wall,
The tide is coming in, I watch the flow
Rise swiftly up where grey-green seaweeds grow.

Close to, below, within a sheltered pool,
In royal purple, jellyfish swim by.
They change in shape and flip themselves and turn
Their milky underbodies to the sky
Where in the distance seabirds wheel and fly.

I gaze, to see the waves advance, retreat -
Some wild, some calm, at one with Nature's law -
And so forever with the changing tides
That beat and batter at the stone-strewn shore
In rhythm with this world forevermore.

A Slippery Trip

Slippery slope a slippery trip
Lolloping over I did a back flip
Into a bush I tried hard to grip
Pulling off pieces and hurting my hip
Passed with alacrity friends start to yip
Echoing voices awake from his kip
Rover who races around me to nip
Yapping and snapping and trying to rip

Trousers and jacket while I give him lip
Rolling and rushing on down to the dip
Into the river I speedily slip
Pissed-off and painful - life gives me the pip.

Beware the Juggernaut

When I was born my mother said,
"I know you have to fly -
But oh my child do please take care
To keep your wings on high.

Beware the juggernaut, my son,
That bears a heavy load,
The lorry and the swift white van
That speed along the road.

Beware the car whose driver bears
A handset by his ear
Who concentrates not on the road
But words that he can hear.

Beware the blaring music
Where, with windows open wide,
They deafen everything nearby
All creatures there outside."

I heeded all my mother's words
And flew around with care.
I floated on the summer breeze;
Was wafted through the air.

I danced with friends in merry crowds.
I buzzed around with glee.
I'd pause to rest among the leaves
That graced each Spring-greened tree.

I revelled in the warming sun -
Was basking in its glow
Forgot the warnings I received
And flew a bit too low.

Along the motorway it zoomed
At speed with glaring lights -
The juggernaut that I should fear.
It struck me in full flight!

I hit the windscreen hard, head on
And there I lay squashed flat.
My fading thoughts my mother's words,
"I think I'll name you Splat!"

Autumn of Life

The bench in the park stands empty -
the old man's not there today.
Sunshine or rain he sat alone
staring ahead with thoughts of his own,
dreaming his life away.

Leaves on the trees are turning.
"Just one more hour near the sky,"
they beg of their host, to no avail,
moistureless, fading, they start to pale
and flutter on down to die.

Birds sing the song of autumn
perched in a multi-hued tree.
"Why has the time flown by so fast?
We wanted summer and warmth to last.
What will our future be?"

Mist-laden evening is calling,
hiding a blood-red sun.
Lengthening shadows betray the day
who wants to rest but cannot stay.
Like all, his time is done.

Fireworks - Madeira New Year 2009

Silhouetted against a cobalt sky
The distant mountain of Madeira stands
Lapped by the waters of a windswept bay
And lit by a thousand glistening lights
Awaiting the midnight chime - the ring of bells
Sounding out the old year - the new one in

All of a sudden the firework flow
That bursts like brilliant flowers
To lap and lick the firmament
Then falls and fades away
The glittering sparks that shoot in fountains
High above the watching Earth
To drop like golden rain into the sea below

Incandescent comets meet and greet
In a cosmic frenzy of flaring fury
While weaving multi-coloured snakes
Curl and crawl their sinuous way
Among the swirling man-made clouds
Which lighten the star-strewn depths

Then clashes and crashes and fiery flashes
And whirling dervishes spiralling high
In flaming circles of orange and gold
And silver and ruby and turquoise and blue

Until without warning punching the air
The machine gun rattle - rat-a-tat-tat-
Cacophony of violent sound

A burst of brightness - a sudden sigh
The indrawn breath - then silence

Blackie

Like a panther he stalks
Sleek black fur shining in the summer sunlight
Paws lightly skimming the new-mown lawn

Green eyes glisten with fixed intent
- A sudden pause as haunches clenched he waits
Claws clasp the sere soil
A tremor of excitement ripples his body
Relentlessly he regards his prey

Unwary sparrows who chirp and chatter
Searching and seeking succulent seeds
Unheeding of the hunter who prowls

A sudden pounce
A silent struggle
A warning cry
A turbulent tumult of birdcall breaking
The flurry of flight - then silence

The victor heads for home
Mouth clenched on still-fluttering feathers
Through the hole in the hedge he slides
To deliver his prey to adoring mistress

Today he lies gaunt body curled
One eye open surveys the world
The black fur browned no longer sleek
No energy no urge to eat
And less to hunt

The birds could come to mock him here
He'd only stare and dream of days
Of strength and vigour now long-gone
And so he rests

The warm earth waits
Sleep well old friend

They Say

They say I look like you mother
I saw the reason why –
In a photo, away on holiday –
I did not have to try
To think who that was posing there;
The face that smiled at me
Was yours in younger years, long past.
I shivered suddenly.

Cockermouth   November 2009

On the roof the soft repeating
Thud, thud, thud of raindrops beating
While the rivers rise and rise to fearsome flow -
And with roar like rabid thunder
rending tree and bridge asunder,
Charge like muddy monsters foaming eyes aglow.

As this awesome wall of water
Surges on in senseless slaughter,
Houses fill with silt and people call for aid.
While through floodtides surging faster,
Devastation and disaster,
The brave and tireless helpers row and wade.

Cockermouth, their vigil keeping,
Must return to black mud seeping
Under doors to ruin all with proud disdain -
Hearing rain that beats and patters,
Seeing life's work lie in tatters,
Begging help that this might not occur again.

BBG Rats (Brilliant Blue G - scientific experimentation)

A face looks out, a face that says,
"Tell me please why I'm lying here.
Is this the way to spend my days,
A prisoner to pain and fear?
Once I ran, was bright and free.
See what science has done to me.

I know that what you do, might aid
In humans, spine recovery -
Injections white-coat men have made
To fill us rats with BBG,
A dye they use in foodstuffs too,
That turns our ears and eyes bright blue.

When you stood there and harmed my spine
I cried with tears I would not show.
I knew your pattern, your design -
To stop the inflammation flow.
This BBG they could reveal
Would help us few white rats to heal.

What of the others? What of the others?
Sisters, cousins, uncles, mothers!

I can move round but oh, so slow.
My blue-tinged paws will turn to pink.
My body mends but they don't know

What right have you to hurt or maim,
Though curing mankind be the aim.

Yet rats are running everywhere
They hide in dustbins, out of sight.
When in the wild they take great care
To mainly hunt for food at night.
We captive rats still have no voice
But rattus-rattus has a choice.

For we are spreading all around -
We watch while humans fight and kill.
We bide our time now underground
And when mankind dies out we will
Take over every city, town -
And tear laboratories down

A Brief Encounter

We had a brief encounter
It happened in the street
I bumped into a man
And dropped my briefcase at his feet.

Out popped all my papers
On which I'd worked so long
The brief I'd been allotted
Which mustn't now go wrong.

We both bent to retrieve them
His umbrella caught my skirt
And pulled it up above my knees
I grabbed hold of his shirt

And hauled myself up looked around
With whirling thoughts in mind
"Dear Madam," said this pleasant man,
"I can see your pert behind.

You have the most delightful briefs
Indeed a wondrous sight
Please grace me with your presence
At a meal for two tonight."

I nodded briefly at him
And tucked his card away
Retrieved my battered briefcase
A most eventful day.

All Hallows Eve

Beneath the stars and midnight sky
Where blind bats flit in mad array
And tawny owls swoop as they fly
With cruel claws to clasp their prey,
In haunts that they alone can know
The witches wheel with eyes aglow.

The moon, a saucer in the sky,
Reflects their shadows on its face,
Like moving pupils on an eye
That glares and stares from high in space;
Cycloptic vision in the night
Reviewing all in eerie light.

Familiars too with bristled coat
Are broomstick-borne. Each feline friend
Spine arched, soars swift to skim and float,
Gaze fixed upon the way they wend;
Their yellow eyes two torchlike flames
That light the way for witches' games.

Whipped treetops toss as wild winds wail
While black-clad beldams dance around.
Tucked tight in beds good folk turn pale
To hear the dread All Hallows sound.
For high above in frenzied flight
The witches whirl in mad delight.

Evening Walk in May

Beside the lightly-greened crop field
On clumped rough ridges of sun-baked soil
Faces warm-wind whipped we make our way
To the newly-emerged small lake

Mayflies skim the hedges and join us
On our journey under the railway
Bent bodies tight squeezed through padlocked
Three-barred gate to the water meadows beyond

Feet squelch on the spongy-soft moss carpet
Dodging the dips of muddy water
Waiting to grab the unwary walker

On firmer parts we crunch upon last year's sere stalks
Settled between a plethora of stinging nettles
In bell-like white flower tempting and treacherous

In the distance among the reeds two Canada geese resting
Ducks swim silently in and out
Between clumps of grey-green grasses
Then flutter up and across the surface quacking as they go

The wind ripples the sun-shimmered water
Sends whispers through the hawthorn hedges
Messages to the mass of rabbits bounding around
Who stop and stare then scuttle swiftly away

Trains clatter past aeroplanes shatter the birdsong
On the towpath far away a cyclist passes
A distant twitcher gazes immobile mute

The walk home by the roadside is a study in colour
White bobbled cow parsley purple convolvulus
Yellow dandelions on the turn
Bluebell heads shaking in their hundreds
Wind music in the making
And clinging close to their new unfurling leaves
Perfectly formed round oak-apples as red as blood.

Grenada Island of Contrasts

Lush greenery lies all around
The bread-fruit and the palm
And gentle waves lap at the shore
In azure coloured calm

Swift seabirds swoop and skim above
Then dive with perfect poise
To seize their prey and sail away
In flap-winged airborne noise

The sometime fields of sugar cane
Stand rippling in the breeze
Surrounding ruined sugar mills
Half-buried in the trees

And bougainvillea burgeons bright
Where washing hung to dry
Bedecks the houses - background to
The people passing by

A hurricane came roaring through
And tore this land apart
It flattened houses crops and trees
And broke its very heart

Now workless wander up and down
And smoke the pipe of peace
It dims the eyes and blurs the mind
But brings some vague release

The waters of the waterfall
Create a foam-tipped pool
Wherein beneath a burning sky
Relief at keeping cool

And birdsong hints at happy days
Before the present blight
When laughter lit the sun-scorched air
And everything was right

The Charge of the White Brigade

Fifty miles, fifty miles,
Fifty miles onward,
Sped down the motorway,
Raced in their hundreds.
Charged on the White Brigade,
Proudly in full parade,
White Van Man, every trade
Valiantly thundered.

Cars to the right of them,
Cars to the left of them,
Cars just in front of them
Bumbled and blundered.
Cared they? No, not a whit.
Shouted, "You silly twit!"
Eyes closed to evil slits
Sped on the Hundreds.

Hallogen blueish lights
Flashed they by day and night.
This was their road, their right,
White Van Man Hundreds.
Sat there with phone by ear
Using one hand to steer -
Bold men that showed no fear
Road spaces plundered.

Lorries to right of them,
Lorries to left of them,
Lorries in front of them
Much louder thundered.
But they cried, "Watch us go!
We'll soon put on a show!"
More timid drivers though,
Worried and wondered.

Oh, what a sight they made!
White Van Man unafraid!
Ton-up and more displayed
By those White Hundreds.
Stopped by police were they
But did not rue the day.
This was their will and way,
Speed crazy Hundreds.
White Van Man Hundreds.